OLD WORLD TREASURES

TEACHER'S MANUAL & ANSWER KEY

Catholic Ve ·*y 4*

St. Jerome Library
WWW.STJEROMELIBRARY.ORG

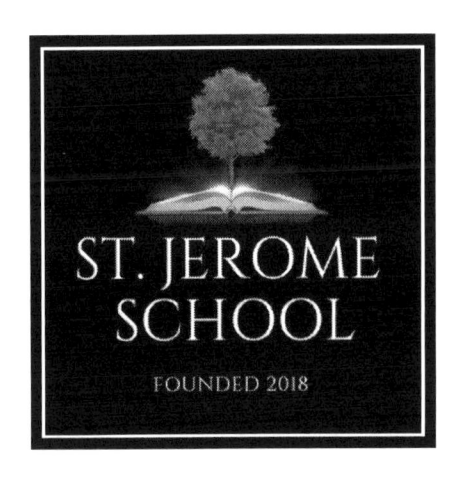

COPYRIGHT ©2019, 2021 BY ST. JEROME LIBRARY PRESS

METAMORA, IN

All Rights Reserved.

No part of this book may be reproduced or transmitted in any form or by any means, electronic or mechanical, including photocopying recording, or by any information storage or retrieval system, without written permission from the publisher.

Teacher's Manual

OLD WORLD TREASURES

FOREWORD

A person who is not familiar with the history of human development cannot claim to be truly educated. The student of today is a man of the world—the whole world—and he cannot comprehend our complex civilization without a knowledge of our heritage.

History is sometimes defined as the "sum of our knowledge about man." American history is only one part of history. America, having received all the worth-while contributions of former civilizations, is related to them. The religious connections of our monotheistic civilization reach back to Judea, even before the time of Christ. Culturally, we in America are indebted to the Greco-Roman civilization as it was passed on by Christian Europe. Racially, American history goes back to the Germanic invaders originally known as barbarians. To the Middle Ages, America owes a debt for many of its political and social traits.

In preparing this series of history textbooks for use in our elementary grades it has been the intention of the authors to give to our American boys and girls an understanding suited to their years of the ancient treasures preserved in our civilization and culture, to imbue them with a greater appreciation of the unity and continuity of all history, and to make them understand their responsibility to pass on, undimmed and unclouded, the light of our Christian civilization.

To accomplish this aim it seemed necessary to place in the first book of the series the material on the European backgrounds of American history. It is only logical to begin history with a study of our ancient heritage. The growth and development of our nation follows then in unbroken sequence. The division of the subject matter for the remaining four books has been carefully planned to avoid repetition, which always robs the story of its freshness and leads to a lack of interest on the part of the student.

In writing OLD WORLD TREASURES, every effort has been made to bring the somewhat obscure and difficult periods of ancient and medieval history within the grasp of a young child. Wherever possible a narrative style has been adopted, and special care has been devoted to the choice of vocabulary. Because of the nature and scope of the material treated, certain difficult historical terms have had to be used. In such instances simple explanations or illustrations have been provided to clarify ideas which might otherwise be confused.

The chronological seems the best approach to the presentation of the matter covered in this book. While only essential dates are given, it would be advisable for the teacher to stress the importance of certain dates. Dates in themselves are more or less meaningless, but some are necessary as a framework for a clearer knowledge and a better understanding of history. The book is organized in terms of the chief "understandings" which the pupil is expected to develop. Each "understanding" is given as a boldface heading. This plan insures a more lucid presentation of only pertinent material. Every incident, date, personality, or movement which is included is focused directly upon some major "understanding."

The material at the end of each chapter includes a diversified group of objective tests which should prove useful for teaching purposes. Much time has been given to the preparation of this material, which is arranged in such a manner as to facilitate its use for actual testing programs if so desired.

The student activities are purposeful in character and thought-provoking. They are designed to make the story which has been read more meaningful. Constant use has been made of the major "understandings" which appear as headings. Thus the things which the pupils "do" relate to fundamental generalizations rather than to details of factual information.

Considerable pride is taken in the fact that the book has been kept to a minimum length. It is a common complaint that textbooks contain more material than pupils are able to master. The authors have made a careful selection of concepts which are not too difficult, and they have presented the materials as interestingly and as concisely as possible.

The school library is recognized as essential to all education. In the field of history there is a rich and varied body of material which will in reality make the pupil relive the story of the past. It will provide an opportunity for him to meet the great men and women who have gone before us in a familiar way and to see the outcome of their actions more clearly than they saw it themselves. The authors have therefore compiled a reading list to accompany many of the chapters in OLD WORLD TREASURES. In a few instances no books are available at the proper grade level.

INTRODUCTION

OBJECTIVES

1. To acquaint the child with the idea that our own great country, the United States of America, did not suddenly spring into existence, but that its development was a gradual process, and that this development was closely connected with and influenced by already existing civilizations.

2. To develop within the child's mind a realization of the fact that no one nation should be regarded as a single, isolated unit, but rather that all nations are mutually interdependent as are the members of the human family.

3. To develop an understanding of the methods used in gaining our knowledge of the past.

WORDS AND TERMS TO UNDERSTAND

SUGGESTED PROCEDURE. Before reading the Introduction place the words listed on page 6 on the blackboard and give an explanation of each. When one of these words occurs in the reading, call it to the child's attention and find out if he really understands its meaning.

Give each child several words to use in original sentences, either as a home assignment or as work for a supervised study period.

Have the children arrange the words in alphabetical order, look up their correct pronunciation in the glossary on pages 254-58, and compile their own simple dictionaries for future reference.

Vary the procedure from chapter to chapter. The following definitions and sentences formed from words listed in the Introduction are illustrative of the types of sentences that can be expected in other chapters:

HISTORY is the name which we give to the story of things that happened long ago.

NATION is a word used when speaking about a group of people who speak the same language, have the same customs, and are closely bound together by common interests and institutions.

Just as grandfather, grandmother, father, mother, brothers, and sisters form one family, so all the nations of the world form the FAMILY OF NATIONS.

The UNITED STATES OF AMERICA is the name which was

given to our country when the thirteen original colonies united to form one great country.

ANCIENT is a word used to describe things which belong to the "long ago."

TOMB is a word meaning a grave or monument for the body of a dead person.

FAR-DISTANT means far, far away. In history we study about people who lived in far-distant lands.

The earliest peoples whom we know about lived or dwelt in caves. They are therefore called CAVE DWELLERS.

CONQUER means to overpower and become the master of another.

A TORCH is a stick of wood burning at one end. The man in the picture on page 5 is carrying a burning TORCH.

FLAMING is another word for burning. A FLAMING fire gives light.

A WEAPON is something with which one fights, such as a gun or a sword.

FERTILE means fruitful. FERTILE soil or FERTILE ground means good soil that will produce much fruit, corn, wheat, or whatever crop has been planted.

GENERATION is a word often used to denote all the people living at one time. The children of a family and their cousins belong to the same GENERATION or period of time. The father, mother, aunts, and uncles belong to another GENERATION. A generation is usually taken to be about thirty-three years.

A CIVILIZED person is the opposite of a savage. A CIVILIZED person is one who has been educated and has learned to do things in a well-ordered way.

The works of literature, the art, and the government of civilized persons form their CIVILIZATION or their CULTURE.

To PRESERVE means to protect or to save from spoiling. When Mother PRESERVES tomatoes or peaches, she cooks them in such a way that they will last a long time without spoiling.

STUDY TESTS FOR REVIEW (page 7)

The tests found at the end of each chapter may be used as assignments or as part of a testing program. The answers given in this manual are intended to be suggestive, not all-inclusive.

1. History is the name given to the study of things which happened long ago.

2. The nations of Europe learned a great deal from the ancient Greeks and Romans.

3. We have learned about the people who lived thousands of years ago from the things which interested students of history found when they dug in places where they believed people had once lived.

4. The earliest people lived a simple life in caves in the colder regions of the earth. They had to hunt for their food and use skins of animals for their clothing. At first they did not know about the use of fire.

5. The first important discovery made by early man was the use of fire. Fire gave man protection against wild animals. Man soon developed new ideas; he began to cook and preserve his food and to make pottery.

6. When we say that men are civilized we mean that they are educated, that they have a definite way of keeping order which is called government, and that they keep records of what they do.

7. The cave dwellers had to hunt for their food and to protect themselves from wild animals. They had no fire with which to keep warm and they knew very little about cooking.

8. Men need some form of government so that they can live in an orderly way and keep peace with one another. If there were no government, everyone would do as he or she pleased, there would be no laws or courts where arguments could be settled, and there would probably be a great deal of trouble and unhappiness.

Things to Do

The topics for discussion, subjects for classroom talks, biographies, posters, and other activities suggested in this section are those that should provide useful classroom activities and practical assignments for the better pupils in the class. Detailed accounts on many topics can be found in the popular children's encyclopedias—the Book of Knowledge, Britannica Junior, Compton's Pictured Encyclopedia, and the World Book Encyclopedia.

Some of the suggested exercises are particularly suited to the development of the child's imaginative ability. Increased interest might be stimulated by offering a prize for the best composition, by arranging a classroom exhibition, or by presenting dramatizations at a general assembly.

It is expected that all pupils keep a history scrapbook. If the pictures from old magazines and books do not satisfy the needs and wants of the children, miniature pictures can be purchased from the following companies:

The Perry Pictures Company, Box B, Malden, Massachusetts
The Colonial Art Company, 1336 West First Street, Oklahoma City 2, Oklahoma
Brown-Robertson Company, Inc., 6 East 34th Street, New York, New York

Interesting materials may be secured from the following institutions which have special collections dealing with the history of ancient civilizations:

Metropolitan Museum of Art, Fifth Avenue at 82nd Street, New York 28, New York
The Henry Huntington Library, San Marino, California
Oriental Institute of the University of Chicago, 1155 East 55th Street, Chicago 37, Illinois

Excellent articles, well illustrated, appear from time to time in the *National Geographic Magazine*, published by the National Geographic Society, Sixteenth and M Streets, N.W., Washington 6, D.C.

CHAPTER 1. TREASURE LANES IN ANCIENT EGYPT

OBJECTIVES

1. To give the children an understanding of the fact that the earliest known civilizations developed in districts which had favorable natural conditions—a warm climate, sufficient water supply, fertile soil.

2. To develop an appreciation of the fact that, though the early peoples lacked many of the comforts and luxuries we now enjoy, their lives were not wholly unlike our own.

3. To develop an understanding of the fact that we have an accurate knowledge of the lives of ancient peoples which is gathered from their own records.

STUDY TESTS FOR REVIEW (pages 26-27)

The answers to be written in the blank spaces are:

1. Africa
2. Nile
3. "black land"
4. hieroglyphics
5. Ra or Re
6. pharaohs
7. 365
8. Rosetta
9. obelisk
10. more than twenty
11. papyrus
12. sphinx
13. pharaoh
14. scribes

PICTURES IN THE CHAPTER

The subject of most of the pictures in the text is obvious from the reading matter. However, it was felt that some of the factual data relating to certain illustrations might be of interest to the teacher and pupils.

Egyptian King Dictating to a Scribe (p. 13). The king wears a type of headdress used to indicate his office. The scepter, in the form of a shepherd's crook, symbolizes his pastoral authority. The scribe, adapted from an Egyptian statue of a scribe, uses his stretched skirt as a table. He writes with a reed, the end of which is split into fibers to form a brush. The palette on the floor holds extra reeds and red and black paint. The king's chair is adapted from the gold-covered chair found in the tomb of King Tutankhamen. In the background is seen the brilliant colored wall painting of the Egyptians.

The Rosetta Stone (p. 14). The section marked in the three parts of the stone and enlarged below are translated: "[There shall be celebrated a festival] from the first day of the month of THOTH, for five days. And [the people] shall wear crowns." The first part of the sentence—There shall be celebrated a festival—is broken off in the hieroglyphs.

Evolution of the Letter S (p. 16). From left to right these are: Egyptian hieroglyphic (representing flowers in a field), Hebrew, Phoenician, Greek, archaic Latin, classic Latin.

Plowing the Fields (p. 17). The crude Egyptian hand plows were drawn by oxen. A man scattering seed preceded the plow and another followed with a stick to prod the oxen and keep them moving (see background).

Procession Entering Temple (p. 19). Note the painted carvings on the front walls (pylon). The doorway is flanked by gigantic statues of the pharaoh builder, by obelisks, flags, and so forth. A long avenue usually led to the temple with a row of crouching rams, sphinxes, or other sacred animals on each side. Beyond the pylon wall may be seen the open courtyard where festivals were held. Beyond that is the pillared hall which led to a smaller dark cell or sanctuary, the room where the god was supposed to reside and which only the priests entered.

Residence of an Egyptian Noble (p. 22). The open upper floor is part of the ventilating system. Pools before the house served as ornaments, reservoirs, and aids to coolness. Young boys had shaven heads except for a spot on the right side where the long "pigtail" grew. Adults usually shaved the head entirely and wore wigs because of the heat and insects.

Mummy Case (p. 25). The open case shows the inner wrappings. Note the amulets attached. The face on the outer case was a formalized portrait of the deceased. Other designs on case are sacred symbols, inscriptions, and so forth.

Reading List

Himes, Vera Carola. *Pepi and the Golden Hawk.* Thomas Y. Crowell Company, 1932. An imaginary account of the childhood adventures of King Pepi of old Egypt. Customs, life, dress, and so forth are historically accurate.

Howard, Alice Woodbury. *The Princess Runs Away: A Story of Egypt in 1900 B.C.* The Macmillan Company, 1934. Information about Egyptian gods, methods of weaving, painting, and so forth are woven into the tale without detracting from its interest or action.

Howard, Alice Woodbury. *Sokar and the Crocodile.* The Macmillan Company, 1928. A fairy story about a little boy in old Egypt.

Meadowcroft, Enid LaMonte. *The Gift of the River.* Thomas Y. Crowell Company, 1937. The history of ancient Egypt, from earliest times to its downfall, presented in attractive form.

Wheeler, Ida W. *Playing with Clay.* The Macmillan Company, 1927. Stories and facts about the making of Egyptian, Greek, Chinese, Dutch, Indian, and other kinds of pots and dishes.

White, Becky. *Bu, the Neanderthal Boy.* Albert Whitman and Company, 1941. A boy's life in western Europe during Neanderthal times.

CHAPTER 2. TREASURES OF THE ANCIENT EAST

Objectives

1. To develop an understanding of the fact that other civilizations were being developed simultaneously with that of Egypt.

2. To show that other nations were also greatly influenced by favorable geographical conditions.

3. To develop an understanding of the fact that varying geographical conditions produced different racial or national characteristics.

Study Tests for Review (pages 39-40)

A. The answers to be written in the blank spaces are:

1-2. Tigris, Euphrates	6. wedge
3-4. Babylonians, Assyrians	7. sun-dried bricks (or brick)
5. Babylonians	8. astronomers

9. Assyrians
10. library
11. Phoenicians
12-13. Israelites, Jews
14. David
15. Moses
16. Jerusalem
17. the one true God (or the true religion)

B. The numbers to be inserted in Column B are:
(25) poems written by King David
(23) the pencil of the Babylonians
(19) given to Moses on Mount Sinai
(22) one who studies the heavens
(24) a fine wood for ships
(20) writing of the ancient Babylonians
(18) laws of the ancient Babylonians

THINGS TO DO

The table suggested in the second question will contain items such as the following:

PEOPLE	GIFT TO CIVILIZATION
The Hebrews	A knowledge of the one true God
	The Ten Commandments
The Phoenicians	Carried Egyptian and Babylonian civilization to others
	Phoenician alphabet
The Assyrians	Great library at Nineveh
	Use of new weapons in warfare
	System of governing colonies
The Babylonians	Code of Hammurabi
	Cuneiform writing
	Knowledge of astronomy
The Egyptians	Egyptian calendar
	Architecture and buildings—pyramids, obelisks, sphinxes
	Use of paper (papyrus), irrigation

PICTURES IN THE CHAPTER

Assyrian Temple (p. 34). The building in the foreground is copied from the palace of King Sargon at Khorsabad (Nineveh). In the background is the Ziggurat temple tower.

Development of Our Alphabet (p. 36). In the top row is the Phoenician alphabet, the grandfather of our alphabet; in the center archaic Latin; and the last row is classic Roman. Only the Phoenician letters which have Latin equivalents are shown in the first row.

READING LIST

Carlisle, Norman and Nelson, Eugene. *Modern Wonder Book of Ships.* John C. Winston Company, 1947. The authors describe ships from the earliest Phoenician and Egyptian craft to the "superliners" of today.

Gere, Frances Kent. *Boy of Babylon.* Longmans, Green and Company, 1941. The life of ancient Babylon and Egypt as seen through the eyes of the son of a Babylonian merchant who was commissioned to buy a rare stone for the king of Egypt.

Lansing, Marion Florence. *Man's Long Climb.* Little, Brown and Company, 1933. Shows how the common things around us had their beginning and were used and developed by man. Houses, fire, pottery, the alphabet, music, money, and numbers are some of the subjects discussed.

CHAPTER 3. PATHWAYS TO GRECIAN TREASURES

OBJECTIVES

1. To develop a clearer concept of the importance of geography in the development of civilization.

2. To develop an understanding of Spartan education; though some of its characteristics are praiseworthy, the main principle—that the child belongs to the state—is wrong.

3. To develop an appreciation of the fact that the fundamental principles of American democracy were developed and upheld by the ancient Athenians.

4. To help the child realize the importance of religion in everyday life; even among the ancient Greeks religion was an all-important factor.

5. To bring out the necessity of cooperation among the various groups within a country and to show that a lack of cooperation tends to weaken the government and pave the way for foreign conquest.

STUDY TESTS FOR REVIEW (pages 64-66)

A. The words to be circled are:

| 1. Yes | 3. Yes | 5. No | 7. Yes | 9. Yes |
| 2. No | 4. No | 6. Yes | 8. No | 10. Yes |

B. The words to be underlined are:

11. Europe
12. courageous
13. the city-state
14. others
15. simple
16. Athens
17. Herodotus
18. Demosthenes
19. many
20. were not

C. The words to be written in the blank spaces are:

21. Persians
22. Athenians (or Greeks)
23. Alexander the Great
24. Philip of Macedon
25. Hellenistic

After the study of a particular nation or country has been completed, teachers may find it helpful to have pupils keep a Who's Who Chart in their notebooks. The one for ancient Greece, for example, would probably contain the following names:

Who's Who in Ancient Greece

Name	Important Fact
Alexander the Great	King of Macedonia who became master of all Greece
Demosthenes	Greek orator who spoke against King Philip of Macedon
Herodotus	Greek writer who is often called the "Father of History"
Homer	Early Greek poet who wrote the *Iliad* and the *Odyssey*
Leonidas	Spartan king who showed great courage during the Battle of Thermopylae
Pericles	Famous Greek statesman whose period was known as the Golden Age of Athens
Phidias	Great Greek sculptor who made the statue of Athena in the Parthenon
Philip of Macedon	King who planned to conquer Greece
Socrates	Famous teacher who lived during the Golden Age of Athens

Pictures in the Chapter

Greek Soldiers (p. 45). The designs decorating the shields (animals, birds, etc.) served to identify the men in battle, similar to the shields and coats of arms of medieval Europe or to the present flags, chevrons, and other military insignia.

Piraeus (p. 49). Piraeus was the harbor of Athens and was located on the coast four miles away. Note the road over the hills to Athens.

Athenian School (p. 52). In this drawing, adapted from a Greek vase, the boy at the left is playing a musical instrument, the boy in the foreground recites from the scroll held by the teacher, the pedagogue (with staff) sits at the right.

The Parthenon (p. 58). The ornaments and details carved in white marble in the restoration of the Parthenon were originally brilliantly colored. The woman in the foreground is wearing the typical Greek costume.

READING LIST

Best, Allena Champlin (pseudonym, Erick Berry). *The Winged Girl of Knossos.* Appleton-Century-Crofts, 1933. A story of the time of King Minos of Crete, records legends of Greece.

Church, Alfred John. *The Iliad for Boys and Girls.* The Macmillan Company, 1923. Told from Homer in simple language.

Church, Alfred John. *The Odyssey for Boys and Girls.* The Macmillan Company, 1925. Told from Homer in simple language.

Hoppin, Frederick Street. *Great Adventures in History and Legend.* David McKay Company, 1940. Stories of Leonidas, king of Sparta, and others.

Snedeker, Caroline Dale. *Theras and His Town.* Doubleday and Company, 1924. An interesting story that may be used as a steppingstone to Homer and Herodotus.

Wheeler, Ida W. *Playing with Clay.* The Macmillan Company, 1927. Stories and facts about the making of Egyptian, Greek, Chinese, Dutch, Indian, and other pots and dishes.

CHAPTER 4. THE ROAD TO ROMAN TREASURES.

OBJECTIVES

1. To strengthen the child's understanding of the importance of geography in the history of any country; that is, of such factors as climate, mountains, rivers, valleys, location of harbors, and the relative position of other nations.

2. To develop the ability to recognize the difference between early Greek and Roman civilization in regard to such things as government, amusements, and so forth.

STUDY TESTS FOR REVIEW (pages 85-86)

A. The correct words are:

1. Alps
2. Adriatic
3. western
4. kings
5. consuls
6. patricians
7-8. patricians, plebeians
9-10. Tiberius Gracchus, Gaius Gracchus
11. Hannibal
12-14. Caesar, Crassus, Pompey

B. Acceptable answers are:

15. general, statesman, ambitious
16. wealthy, weak
17. general, ambitious
18. unwise, cruel, traitor
19. unwise, cruel, traitor
20. general, ambitious

PICTURES IN THE CHAPTER

Gladiatorial Contest (p. 74). The view is from the gallery of the amphitheater, with the emperor's box on the right. The shadows on the ground of the arena are thrown by huge awnings stretched over the galleries to protect the spectators from the sun.

Caesar in Britain (p. 80). Note the whitewashed cliffs of Dover, where the Roman soldiers landed in Britain.

CHAPTER 5. OUR GREATEST TREASURE

OBJECTIVES

1. To develop within the child's heart a deep and lasting love of our blessed Lord, based on a realization of His love for us.
2. To awaken a consciousness that Christ loved *all* men and wishes us to love *all*.
3. To strengthen the virtue of obedience.
4. To enkindle respect for *all* lawfully constituted authority.

STUDY TESTS FOR REVIEW (page 100)

Acceptable answers are:

1. "If you love me, keep my commandments" (John 14:15). "He who has my commandments and keeps them, he it is who loves me" (John 14:21). "If you keep my commandments you will abide in my love, as I also have kept my Father's commandments, and abide in his love" (John 15:10). "One there is who is good, and he is God. But if thou wilt enter into life, keep the commandments" (Matthew 19:17). "Not everyone who says to me, 'Lord, Lord,' shall enter the

kingdom of heaven; but he who does the will of my Father in heaven shall enter the kingdom of heaven" (Matthew 7:21).

2. Christ cured the blind (Matthew 9:27-31; 12:22; 20:30-34; Mark 8:22-26; 10:46-52; Luke 18:35-43; John 9:1-7), the deaf (Mark 7:32-35), lepers (Matthew 8:2-3; Luke 17:12-19), paralytics (Matthew 8:5-13; 9:2-8), those suffering from fever (Luke 4:38-39; John 4:46-53), praised the works of mercy (Matthew 25:35-40), the Good Samaritan (Luke 10:30-37).

3. (a) True happiness does not consist in great riches. (b) We must be ready to do penance and to deny ourselves. (c) We must obey God and all who have authority over us. (d) We must love and help the sick, the poor, those in sorrow and in need.

4. Christ's death is the greatest proof of His love for us.

Reading List

Beebe, Catherine. *Story of Jesus for Boys and Girls*. Bruce Publishing Company, 1945. A life of Jesus in clear, short sentences and simple language.

Hunt, Marigold. *A Life of Our Lord for Children*. Sheed and Ward, 1944. The story of the great King who came down from heaven to earth, and the necessity of His coming.

Loewenstein, Prince Hubertus. *The Child and the Emperor*. The Macmillan Company, 1945. This beautiful legend tells the story of the meeting of the young Jesus, the humble stranger from Galilee, and the mighty Augustus, ruler of the world.

Petersham, Maud and Petersham, Miska. *The Christ Child as Told by Matthew and Luke*. Catholic edition. Doubleday and Company, 1931. The Christmas story, beginning with the prophecies and ending with the finding of Christ in the temple.

Price, Olive M. *Miracle by the Sea*. McGraw-Hill Book Company, 1947. The author has the special ability to make the past seem real and very close. This story is about the little boy who provided the loaves and fishes when Christ performed the miracle and fed the multitude.

Thompson, Blanche Jennings, editor. *Bible Children*. Dodd, Mead and Company, 1937. A charming book which includes Bible stories in which children appear.

CHAPTER 6. THE CHURCH AND EVERLASTING TREASURES

Objectives

1. To foster a strong love for our holy mother the Church, based on a lively faith that she is the mouthpiece of Christ, spreading His teachings to all nations, and guiding all to their goal of eternal salvation.

Study Tests for Review (pages 113-14)

A. Acceptable answers for the blank spaces are:

1. teach us the way to heaven
2. Pentecost (Whit Sunday)
3. St. Peter
4. Pope Pius XII
5. Constantine
6. St. Ambrose
7. Constantine
8. Paul

B. The numbers to be inserted in Column B are:

(13) ordered the Scriptures to be burned
(12) burial places of early Christians
(10) converted while on his way to persecute the Christians
(11) Edict of Milan
(9) first persecution of the Christians

Who's Who in the Early History of the Church

Name	Important Fact
St. Agnes	A little Roman girl about thirteen years old who was martyred because she loved Christ
St. Ambrose	The great bishop of Milan who baptized St. Augustine
Constantine	The Roman emperor who, by the Edict of Milan, granted freedom of worship to the Christians
Diocletian	A Roman emperor who persecuted the Christians and ordered the Scriptures to be burned
St. Felicitas	A slave girl, one of the early martyrs, who was thrown to the wild beasts because she was a Christian
St. Lawrence	One of the early Christian martyrs who, according to tradition, was roasted on a gridiron
Maxentius	The rival of Constantine who was drowned in the Tiber River

NAME	IMPORTANT FACT
Nero	The first of the Roman emperors who persecuted the Christians; St. Peter and St. Paul martyred at this time
St. Paul	The "Apostle of the Gentiles" who was beheaded at about the same time that St. Peter was crucified
St. Perpetua	The companion of St. Felicitas, who was also martyred because she was a Christian
St. Peter	The "Prince of the Apostles," crucified head downward during the persecution of Nero, about 67 A.D.
Saul	The name used by the great St. Paul before he became a Christian
St. Sebastian	A Roman martyr who, according to tradition, was shot to death with arrows
St. Tarsicius	A Roman boy who suffered a violent death rather than let a mob treat with disrespect the Blessed Sacrament which he was carrying to some Christians in prison
Theodosius	The Roman emperor during whose reign Christianity became the religion of the Empire

READING LIST

Homan, Helen W. *Little St. Agnes*. Longmans, Green and Company, 1938. A favorite saint of little children, written with simplicity.

Shore, Maxine and Oblinger, Milo M. *The Slave Who Dreamed*. Westminster Press, 1944. Lucius learns of Christianity from the grandson of Joseph of Arimathea and adopts the ways of the Christians after St. Paul helps him to escape from his cruel masters.

CHAPTER 7. ROMAN TREASURES STILL ENRICH US

OBJECTIVES

1. To awaken within the child's mind a consciousness that the foundations of many things which we prize in our own civilization were laid in the days of the early Romans.

2. Among the Roman gifts which we treasure are our religion, our language and literature, our ideas of government, and our legal system.

STUDY TESTS FOR REVIEW (pages 126-27)

Acceptable answers are:

1. Christianity   2. Latin

3. ancient Greeks
4. Pliny
5-6. buildings, bridges, roads
7. roads, bridges
8. Law (Legal system)
9. Church
10. barbarians
11. 476
12. thousand

WHO'S WHO IN EARLY ROME

NAME	IMPORTANT FACT
Antony	The rival and enemy of Octavian
Augustus	The ruler of the Roman world at the time that Christ was born in Bethlehem
Brutus	A Roman senator who plotted the death of Julius Caesar
Caesar	A great general and statesman who was master of Rome after the death of Crassus and Pompey
Cassius	An enemy of Caesar who, with Brutus, brought about his death
Cicero	The greatest Roman orator and a famous writer
Crassus	A member of the First Triumvirate and a rival of Julius Caesar
Gaius Gracchus and Tiberius Gracchus	Brothers who became leaders of the plebeians and wanted laws to be passed that would help the plebeians
Hannibal	The great leader of the Carthaginians in the Punic wars
Horace	A well-known Roman poet who lived during the reign of Augustus
Huns	The barbarians who came into Europe from central Asia
Justinian	A great Roman emperor who ordered all Roman laws to be collected; collection called the "Body of the Civil Law"
Octavian	The name of Emperor Augustus
Pliny	A Roman who was one of the first great letter writers
Pompey	A member of the First Triumvirate and a rival of Julius Caesar
Remus and Romulus	Twin brothers who, according to legend, were the founders of the city of Rome

Name	Important Fact
Tarquins	The name of the last three kings in the history of early Rome
Vergil	A well-known Roman poet who lived in the days of Emperor Augustus
Vespasian	The Roman emperor who built the Colosseum in ancient Rome

PICTURE IN THE CHAPTER

Roman Bridge (p. 117). The Pont du Gard, Nimes, as it stands today. The upper part served as an aqueduct, the lower level as a bridge.

SEMESTER TEST

[Based on material covered in Chapters 1-7]

A. Before each item in Column B write the number of the item in Column A which is most closely connected with it.

COLUMN A	COLUMN B
1. Solomon	( ) a Spartan king who led the Greeks in the Battle of Thermopylae
2. Leonidas	( ) the first Roman emperor to persecute the Christians
3. Homer	( ) the father of Alexander the Great
4. Phidias	( ) the legendary founders of Rome
5. Philip of Macedon	( ) issued the Edict of Milan
6. Hannibal	( ) the "Father of History"
7. Constantine	( ) built a temple in Jerusalem
8. Romulus and Remus	( ) the great poet of early Greece
9. Herodotus	( ) the sculptor of the statue of Athena
10. Nero	( ) the great leader of the Carthaginians in the Punic wars

B. Complete the following sentences by writing the correct words in the blank spaces.

11. The .... is the key to the Egyptian hieroglyphics.
12. The pyramid of .... is very famous.
13. An Egyptian ruler was called a ....
14. The writing of the ancient Babylonians was called .... writing.
15. Carthage was a famous colony of the ....

TEACHER'S MANUAL

16. .... was a teacher who helped the Greeks to think well by asking them questions.

17. Jesus Christ was born during the reign of Emperor ....

18. A man traveling in the army of .... found the key to the Egyptian hieroglyphics.

19. The Babylonians were conquered by the ....

20. The Assyrians built an important library at ....

21. .... was an important city in ancient Phoenicia.

22. Slaves in ancient Sparta were called ....

23. The Greeks held the .... every four years in honor of Zeus.

24. The new culture built up by Alexander the Great is called ....

25. St. Peter and St. Paul were martyred during the persecutions of Emperor ....

C. Draw a line under the words that complete the following sentences correctly.

26. The pyramids were (temples, tombs, storehouses).

27. Egyptian writings were in the form of (books, pamphlets, scrolls).

28. The ancient Egyptians worshiped (Zeus, the sun, fire).

29. The ancient Egyptian writing is called (hieroglyphics, cuneiform, phonetic).

30. The Babylonians wrote on (paper, clay tablets, papyrus).

31. The famous Hebrew who wrote the Psalms was (Solomon, Moses, David).

32. The Spartans liked (athletics, music, painting).

33. Marathon was a (battle, dance, general).

34. Pericles was a (poet, dancer, statesman).

35. Military training was an important part in the education of the youth in (Sparta, Athens, Thebes).

36. Athenian girls were taught (at home, in schools for boys and girls, in parochial schools).

37. The Greek orator whose speeches were known as the "Philippics" was (Pericles, Demosthenes, Themistocles).

38. The best harbors of Italy are on the (east, west, north) coast.

39. The Roman emperor who became a Christian after he won an important battle was (Constantine, Nero, Maxentius).

40. Crassus was a (rival of Caesar, strong general, leader of the plebeians).

20   OLD WORLD TREASURES

D. Each of the following questions can be answered by Yes or No. Draw a circle around the correct answer.

41. Did the ancient Greeks worship only one God?   Yes No
42. Were the poor people in Greece treated in a kindly manner by their masters?   Yes No
43. Did the Assyrians know how to rule a large empire? Yes No
44. Were the Phoenicians good shipbuilders?   Yes No
45. Did the ancient Greeks ever see snow?   Yes No
46. Was ancient Greece a strongly united country?   Yes No
47. Did the ancient Spartans spend much time in training the characters of their young boys and girls?   Yes No
48. Did Hannibal's father teach him to love the Romans? Yes No
49. Did Julius Caesar have any enemies among the Roman senators?   Yes No
50. Did our Lord prepare the apostles for the sufferings they would have to endure?   Yes No

E. Write the answers to the following questions in the space provided.

51. Where were the Roman gladiatorial combats held? ....
52. Where did the Roman chariot races take place? ....
53. What was the name of the poorer people in early Roman society? ....
54. What country is sometimes called "the Gift of the Nile"? ....
55. In what city does the largest Egyptian obelisk about which we have any knowledge now stand? ....
56. What was the name of the Athenian market place? ....
57. From what language does the word "democracy" come? ....
58. What is the name of the great hill overlooking the plain of Athens? ....
59. Where was the first great battle between the ancient Greeks and the Persians fought? ....
60. What is the name given to the wars fought between ancient Rome and Carthage? ....
61. What is the old name for the country we now call France? ....
62. Who was the first apostle to preach in public? ....
63. Who is called the "Apostle of the Gentiles"? ....

64. Who was the Roman emperor who closed the pagan temples? ....
65. Who were the barbarians from central Asia whom the Romans were too weak to keep out of the Empire? ....

F. Here is a list of ancient countries and the names of some famous men. Write on the line opposite his name the name of the country, chosen from this list, with which each of the men is most closely connected.

| Egypt | Greece | Carthage | Palestine |
| Phoenicia | Rome | Babylonia | Macedonia |

66. Diocletian ....
67. Theodosius ....
68. Philip ....
69. Zeus ....
70. Khufu ....
71. Hammurabi ....
72. King David ....
73. Pericles ....
74. Tarquins ....
75. Hannibal ....
76. Julius Caesar ....
77. St. Agnes ....
78. Justinian ....
79. Alexander the Great ....
80. Phidias ....

G. Complete the following sentences by filling in the blank spaces with words taken from this list. A word may be used more than once if necessary.

Mediterranean	Apennine	Europe	Rhone
Adriatic	Lebanon	Africa	Tiber
Persian	Alps	Sicily	Po

81. The Nile River empties into the .... Sea.
82. The .... Mountains are in Phoenicia.
83. The body of water on the east of Italy is called the .... Sea.
84. The large island off the tip of Italy is ....
85. Italy is protected on the north by the .... Mountains.
86. Greece is in the continent of ....
87. The .... Mountains are the backbone of Italy.
88. Rome is on the .... River.
89. Hannibal crossed the .... River in France.
90. The Tigris and Euphrates rivers flow into the .... Gulf.

H. The most important peoples of ancient times are listed in Column A. Before each item in Column B write the number of the peoples with which it is most closely connected.

Column A   Column B
91. Phoenicians   ( ) built many wonderful roads

OLD WORLD TREASURES

Column A	Column B
92. Egyptians	( ) chief enemies of the ancient Greeks
93. Persians	( ) held religious festivals called Olympic Games
94. Babylonians	( ) Hannibal was their famous leader
95. Hebrews	( ) carried the alphabet to different parts of Europe, Asia, and Africa
96. Carthaginians	( ) ruled by Alexander the Great
97. Greeks	( ) built the pyramids
98. Macedonians	( ) built their capital at Nineveh on the Tigris
99. Romans	( ) Hammurabi was their famous lawgiver
100. Assyrians	( ) gave the world the knowledge of the one true God

Answers to Semester Test

A. The numbers to be inserted in Column B are:

(2) a Spartan king who led the Greeks in the Battle of Thermopylae
(10) the first Roman emperor to persecute the Christians
(5) the father of Alexander the Great
(8) the legendary founders of Rome
(7) issued the Edict of Milan
(9) the "Father of History"
(1) built a temple in Jerusalem
(3) the great poet of early Greece
(4) the sculptor of the statue of Athena
(6) the great leader of the Carthaginians in the Punic wars

B. The words to be written in the blank spaces are:

11. Rosetta Stone
12. Khufu
13. pharaoh
14. cuneiform
15. Phoenicians
16. Socrates
17. Augustus
18. Napoleon
19. Assyrians
20. Nineveh
21. Tyre, Sidon
22. helots
23. Olympic Games
24. Hellenistic
25. Nero

C. The words to be underlined are:

26. tombs
27. scrolls
28. the sun
29. hieroglyphics
30. clay tablets
31. David
32. athletics
33. battle
34. statesman
35. Sparta
36. at home
37. Demosthenes
38. west
39. Constantine
40. rival of Caesar

D. The words to be circled are:

41. No   43. Yes   45. Yes   47. No   49. Yes
42. No   44. Yes   46. No   48. No   50. Yes

E. Acceptable answers are:

51. Colosseum   56. Agora   61. Gaul
52. Circus Maximus   57. Greek   62. St. Peter
53. plebeians   58. Acropolis   63. St. Paul
54. Egypt   59. Marathon   64. Theodosius
55. Rome   60. Punic   65. Huns

F. Acceptable answers are:

66. Rome   71. Babylonia   76. Rome
67. Rome   72. Palestine   77. Rome
68. Macedonia   73. Greece   78. Rome
69. Greece   74. Rome   79. Macedonia
70. Egypt   75. Carthage   80. Greece

G. The words to be written in the blank spaces are:

81. Mediterranean   85. Alps   88. Tiber
82. Lebanon   86. Europe   89. Rhone
83. Adriatic   87. Apennine   90. Persian
84. Sicily

H. The numbers to be inserted in Column B are:

(99) built many wonderful roads
(93) chief enemies of the ancient Greeks
(97) held religious festivals called Olympic Games
(96) Hannibal was their famous leader
(91) carried the alphabet to different parts of Europe, Asia, and Africa
(98) ruled by Alexander the Great
(92) built the pyramids
(100) built their capital at Nineveh on the Tigris
(94) Hammurabi was their famous lawgiver
(95) gave the world the knowledge of the one true God

CHAPTER 8. ANCIENT TREASURES ALMOST DESTROYED

OBJECTIVES

1. To develop an understanding of the fact that the barbarian invasions resulted from conditions both within and without the Empire.

2. To form a clear concept of the nature of the Huns.

3. To foster an appreciation of the historic fact that the Teutonic invaders were the founders of many great European nations.

STUDY TESTS FOR REVIEW (pages 138-39)

The words to be written in the blank spaces are:

1. Huns
2. Huns
3. Alaric
4-5. Visigoths, Vandals
6-7. Clovis, Clotilde
8. Teutonic (German, barbarian)
9. St. Remi
10. "do-nothing kings"
11. Charles Martel
12. Pepin

PICTURE IN THE CHAPTER

Baptism of Clovis (p. 135). Illustration shows interior of a typical French baptistery of the period, a small building near a cathedral or church. The baptistery was usually octangular or round in shape with the font (pool) in the center under a canopy with curtained sides.

READING LIST

Cather, Katherine Dunlap. *Girlhood Stories of Famous Women*. Appleton-Century-Crofts, 1924. Contains stories of Clotilde of Burgundy and Elizabeth of England.

CHAPTER 9. MOHAMMED THREATENS OUR TREASURES

OBJECTIVES

1. To develop an understanding of the geographical relation of the Arabian peninsula to the other centers of civilization about which the pupil has already studied.

2. To arouse interest in studying the origin and spread of Mohammedanism.

3. To give the child a true appreciation of Mohammedan contributions to culture and civilization.

STUDY TESTS FOR REVIEW (pages 146-47)

A. The words to be underlined are:
1. south 2. east 3. Spain 4. India 5. north

B. The dates to be written in the blank spaces are:
6. 732   7. 622   8. 1492   9. 632[1]   10. 711

---
[1] This date is not actually given, but the child should be able to figure it out for himself. See pages 143, 144.

C. The words to be written in the blank spaces are:
11. caravans
12. Koran
13. Mecca
14-17. Mecca, Medina, 622, Hegira
18. Hegira
19-20. Spain, Moors (Mohammedans)

CHAPTER 10. THE MONKS SAVE OUR TREASURES

Objectives

1. To develop a clear understanding that it was the work of the Catholic Church among the barbarians which preserved what was best in their customs and raised them to a higher level of civilization and culture.

2. To give an understanding that the Church is for ALL, and that her labors are not limited by race or color.

3. To foster an appreciation of the fact that the Church numbers people from ALL races in the calendar of the saints.

Study Tests for Review (pages 104-66)

A. The words to be written in the blank spaces are:
1. St. Augustine
2. St. Ambrose
3. Italy
4. St. Benedict
5. England
6. Egypt
7. Pope Gregory the Great

B. Acceptable answers are:
8-10. poverty, chastity, obedience
11-12. monastery, common
13. abbot
14. Scriptures (Bible)
15. priests
16. Divine Office
17. Scriptures
18. rules

C. The numbers to be inserted in Column B are:
(21) apostle of the Irish
(26) the first hermit
(28) queen of England
(27) "Father of Western Monasticism"
(25) converted the English
(20) bishop of Milan
(22) a sinner who became a great saint
(24) converted the Germans
(19) established monasteries in the desert
(23) mother of St. Augustine

The Apostles of the Nations

Nation	Apostle
Roman Empire	St. Peter and St. Paul
Franks	St. Remi
Northern Africa	St. Augustine of Hippo
Ireland	St. Patrick
England	St. Augustine of Canterbury
Germany	St. Boniface
Slavs	St. Cyril and St. Methodius

Who's Who in the Calendar of the Saints

Saint	Nation	Feast Day
St. Agnes	Rome	January 21
St. Ambrose	Italy	December 7
St. Anthony of the Desert	Egypt	January 17
St. Augustine of Canterbury	England	May 28
St. Augustine of Hippo	Africa	August 28
St. Benedict	Italy	March 21
St. Bernard	France	August 20
St. Boniface	Germany	June 5
St. Clare	Italy	August 12
St. Cyril	Slavs	July 7
St. Dominic	Spain	August 4
St. Elizabeth	Hungary	November 19
St. Felicitas	Africa	March 6
St. Francis of Assisi	Italy	October 4
St. Gregory the Great	Italy	March 12
St. Joan of Arc	France	May 30
St. John the Evangelist	Jerusalem	December 27
St. Joseph	Jerusalem	March 19
St. Lawrence	Rome	August 10
St. Louis	France	August 25
St. Mary Magdalene	Jerusalem	July 22
St. Methodius	Slavs	July 7
St. Monica	Africa	May 4
St. Pachomius	Egypt	May 9
St. Patrick	Ireland	March 17
St. Paul	Rome	June 29
St. Perpetua	Africa	March 6
St. Peter	Rome (Jerusalem)	June 29

Saint	Nation	Feast Day
St. Remi (Remigius)	France	October 1
St. Sebastian	Rome	January 20
St. Tarsicius	Rome	August 15

Pictures in the Chapter

St. Anthony and Monks (p. 150). In the background are the huts of the monks scattered over the desert at about calling distance from one another.

Monks of St. Pachomius (p. 151). These monks spent considerable time working for the community. Note that the huts are much closer together.

St. Patrick (p. 155). He uses a shamrock (trefoil) to explain the Holy Trinity.

Medieval Monastery (p. 159). The arrangement of the abbey is based on that of the ancient Fountains Abbey, Yorkshire, England. Buildings with monastic cells and workshops surround the central cloister. On the side of the cloister next to the river is the refectory and kitchen; to the left, connected by a bridge, are guest houses; to the right is the infirmary. The abbey church or minster is located at the rear of the other buildings. Part of the wall enclosing the abbey lands can be seen in the lower left.

Reading List

Stein, Evaleen. *Gabriel and the Hour Book.* L. C. Page and Company, 1906. The story of a French peasant boy who helped Brother Stephen illuminate a book.

Windeatt, Mary Fabyan. *Hero of the Hills.* Sheed and Ward, 1943. A life of St. Benedict.

Windeatt, Mary Fabyan. *Northern Lights.* Sheed and Ward, 1945. The story of St. Hyacinth of Poland who preached and performed miracles in Poland, Prussia, Lithuania, Latvia, and Russia.

CHAPTER 11. CHARLEMAGNE PROTECTS OUR TREASURES

Objectives

1. To develop clearly the concept that a good ruler is one who works, not for his own selfish interests, but for the welfare of his subjects; therefore, one who makes lasting contributions to civilization.

2. To emphasize the great extent of Charlemagne's empire and the importance of the fact that at his death no one individual ruler was capable of holding it together.

3. To show how the rise of three of the leading nations of Europe can be traced to the divisions of Charlemagne's kingdom.

Study Tests for Review (pages 175-76)

A. The words to be written in the blank spaces are:

1. Middle Ages
2. Alcuin
3. Forty-four years
4. Fourteen years
5. Saxons
6. Treaty of Verdun
7. Lothair
8. The pope
9. Rollo
10. Norsemen (Northmen)

B. Acceptable answers are:

11-13. Norway, Sweden, Denmark
14. Normans
15-17. Christmas, 800, Leo III
18-19. Lombards, Papal
20-22. Northmen, Hungarians, Saracens

Picture in the Chapter

Illuminated Manuscript (p. 168). The text is from page 170 and shows how the page might have looked if it were produced about the beginning of the ninth century. The type of lettering, border decoration, color, and use of gold are all typical of the period. The illumination in the capital *C* shows how the monks did this work. The bracket above his writing desk holds the book he is copying. Inkwells and colors in horns are attached to the side and base of his desk. He works on a single sheet of parchment and a weight hangs by a cord over the manuscript to keep it flat. The reed or quill pen is in his right hand; in the left is a scraper to smooth rough spots in the parchment or to remove errors when alterations are necessary.

Reading List

Burglon, Nora. *Children of the Soil: A Story of Scandinavia.* Doubleday and Company, 1932. A story of child life on a farm on the coast of Sweden. The fairy element adds interest to the story, which tells something of the home life and industries of Sweden.

Chamoud, Simone. *Picture Tales from the French.* J. B. Lippincott Company, 1933. Old legends of Brittany and Gascony.

Hyde, Mark Powell. *The Singing Sword: The Story of Sir Ogier, the Dane.* Little, Brown and Company, 1930. A tale of the time of

Charlemagne wherein Ogier the Dane distinguishes himself and is knighted at an early age.

CHAPTER 12. TREASURES IN ENGLAND

OBJECTIVES

1. To arouse the children to an understanding of the fact that many Englishmen could trace their ancestry back to those whom we have called the barbarians from northern Europe, or to the Normans in France.

2. To awaken within the children an appreciation of the close relationship existing between the culture and civilization of England and that of European countries.

STUDY TESTS FOR REVIEW (pages 185-87)

A. The words to be circled are:

1. No	6. Yes	10. No	14. No
2. Yes	7. No	11. Yes	15. Yes
3. No	8. No	12. Yes	16. No
4. Yes	9. No	13. No	17. Yes
5. No			

Teachers should not be satisfied with a mere *yes* or *no* in answer to these seventeen questions. To avoid guessing on the part of pupils, the teacher may require complete sentences, as:

1. No, Christ was born after the death of Julius Caesar.

2. Yes, they all spoke the same language and developed the same type of civilization.

3. No, they did not get on well together in England and set up separate kingdoms.

4. Yes, they were afraid that the Danes, who were fierce and cruel, would take their lands away from them.

5. No, the Danes did not keep the promise they made to King Alfred.

6. Yes, Alfred deserves to be called Alfred the Great because of all the good he did for his people.

7. No, Alfred ruled only over Wessex, the kingdom of the West Saxons.

8. No, King Ethelred fled from England because he could not drive back the Danes.

9. No, King Edward was very pious, but he was easily led by others.

10. No, King Edward had no children.

11. Yes, William, duke of Normandy, became King William I of England in 1066. He is known as William the Conqueror.

12. Yes, William the Conqueror strengthened the power of the English king when all the nobles swore that they would be loyal to him.

13. No, after the Norman Conquest the French language was spoken at the English court.

14. No, William gave important official positions to his Norman followers.

15. Yes, the Norman Conquest, one of the greatest events in the history of Europe, brought many changes to England.

16. No, the Domesday Book was a record of the first census taken in England.

17. Yes, William the Conqueror was kind and generous to the monks.

B. Acceptable answers are:

18-19. weak, undecided	24-25. warlike, cruel, strong
20-21. pious, weak	26-27. young, just, good, wise,
22-23. brave, strong, good, wise, clever	learned, brave, strong

Reading List

Baldwin, James. *Fifty Famous Stories Retold.* American Book Company, 1924. Historical legends of Alfred the Great and others.

Comstock, Harriet Theresa. *A Boy of a Thousand Years Ago.* Lothrop, Lee and Shepard Company, 1902. A story of the home life and training of Alfred the Great and of his later successes and failures.

Tappan, Eva March. *In the Days of Alfred the Great.* Lothrop, Lee and Shepard Company, 1900.

Tappan, Eva March. *In the Days of William the Conqueror.* Lothrop, Lee and Shepard Company.

CHAPTER 13. TREASURES IN LANDS AND CASTLES

Objectives

1. To emphasize the great difference existing between the customs and practices of the Middle Ages and those of our own times.

2. To stress the "knightly" characteristics of a world influenced

by the Church; ideals which today are fostered and upheld primarily by the Church.

3. To give the pupils an understanding of the simplicity of life in the Middle Ages as compared with our complex modern society.

STUDY TESTS FOR REVIEW (pages 197-99)

A. The numbers to be inserted in Column B are:

(9) knightly code of manners
(5) great stone houses in feudal times
(1) those who owned the land and ruled in feudal days
(6) the ceremony in which a vassal bound himself to his lord
(15) wandering singers
(12) that part of a castle which was a place of special safety
(2) those who held land in return for certain services
(10) a young boy learning to be a knight
(13) material used to make armor in feudal times
(3) those who tilled the land in feudal times
(4) the large estates belonging to the lords
(7) the blow on the shoulder given in the ceremony of knighthood
(8) a big ditch dug around the castle wall for safety
(14) the price paid to free a lord who was prisoner
(11) a battle fought according to definite rules

B. The words to be underlined are:

| 16. did not | 18. sometimes | 20. small |
| 17. were not | 19. page | 21. twenty-one |

PICTURE IN THE CHAPTER

Medieval Castle (p. 194). This is a composite of typical castles of the period. Round building to the left of the drawbridge over the moat is the "donjon." The large squarish building in the upper right is the "tower" or "keep." The long building running along the walls in the right foreground is the "great hall." The chapel is to the left of the tower. Other small buildings within the ramparts are workshops, stables, and so forth. Outside the castle moat are the small houses of the peasants, the village buildings, fields, etc.—all within the enclosure of lesser walls.

READING LIST

Buff, Mary Marsh and Buff, Conrad. *Kobi, a Boy of Switzerland.* Viking Press, 1939. Pictures castle life.

Gray, Elizabeth Janet. *Adam of the Road.* Viking Press, 1942. An appealing picture of medieval life.

Lansing, Marion Florence. *Page, Esquire, and Knight: A Book of Chivalry.* Ginn and Company, 1910. Tales of King Arthur, Charlemagne, and other heroes.

Lownsbery, Eloise. *Out of the Flame.* Longmans, Green and Company, 1931. A fine story of the life of Pierre de Bayard as page and squire at the court of Francis I, early in the sixteenth century. Training for knighthood, tournaments, and so forth well described.

CHAPTER 14. EXCHANGING TREASURES

OBJECTIVES

1. To develop an understanding of the fact that our modern system of trading is the result of a gradual development.

2. To give a knowledge of the difficulties and inconveniences of early trade and communication as contrasted with modern methods.

3. To show that the medieval guilds were forerunners of modern trade unions.

STUDY TESTS FOR REVIEW (pages 210-11)

A. The words to be underlined are:

1. was
2. little
3. Belgium
4. Normans
5. Genoa
6. Baltic Sea
7. often
8. an apprentice
9. very poor
10. did

B. The words to be written in the blank spaces are:

Venice	Marco	Venice
Nicolo Polo	father	treasures (jewels)
Maffeo Polo	uncle	prisoner
Black	Cathay	Genoa
Kublai Khan	Cathay	*The Travels of Marco Polo*
Cathay	wealthy	Christopher Columbus

PICTURE IN THE CHAPTER

Medieval Shop (p. 203). The craftsman's home and shop were one. A window or counter opening into the street provided a place to display and sell the wares made in the shop. An apprentice, who would also live in the house, can be seen working inside as the master attends customers.

Reading List

Cather, Katherine Dunlap. *The Castle of the Hawk.* Appleton-Century-Crofts, 1927. A story that tells of clockmaking in Switzerland during the time of Count Rudolph of Habsburg. The book throws light on the work of the guilds of the Middle Ages.

Coffman, Ramon Peyton and Goodman, Nathan Gerson. *Famous Explorers for Boys and Girls.* A. S. Barnes and Company, 1942. Stories of Marco Polo and others.

Gilchrist, Marie Emilie and Ögle, Lucille. *Rolling Along through the Centuries.* Longmans, Green and Company, 1937. The evolution of land travel, from the making of wheels in primitive times to modern streamline trains and automobiles. Profusely illustrated.

Rue, Flora Clark. *From Barter to Money.* Row, Peterson and Company, 1941. One of the books in the basic social education series.

Smith, Nila Banton and others. *Distant Doorways.* Unit Activity Reading Series, Book 4. Silver, Burdett Company, 1940. Stories of Marco Polo and others.

Wiese, Kurt. *The Chinese Ink Stick.* Doubleday and Company, 1929. An unusual book, which tells in an interesting way about Chinese writing, pictures, and customs.

CHAPTER 15. WINNING BACK LOST TREASURES

Objectives

1. To develop an understanding of the importance of the Crusades in the development of the history of Europe.

2. To show that the Crusades helped to spread knowledge, and that they fostered an interchange of ideas and ideals between East and West.

3. To awaken within the child a realization that this closer communication between East and West led to an increase in trade and was one of the causes of the desire to find a new route to the East.

Study Tests for Review (pages 218-20)

A. The numbers to be inserted in Column B are:
(3) the great leader of the Turks
(8) king of England who joined a crusade
(5) the pope who organized the First Crusade
(2) king of France who led two crusades
(4) king drowned in Asia Minor
(9) took the title of "Defender of the Holy Sepulcher"

(6) preached the Second Crusade
(1) led an undisciplined group of pilgrims to the Holy Land
(7) king of France who went on the Third Crusade

B. The correct answers are:

10. True	13. True	16. True
11. True	14. False	17. False
12. False	15. True	18. True

The chart made for the Crusades may contain any of the following:

LEADERS: Godfrey of Bouillon, King Frederick Barbarossa, King Philip Augustus, King Richard the Lion-Hearted, St. Louis. (Note that Peter the Hermit did not lead a real army and his journey was not considered a crusade.)

CAUSES: (1) To free the Holy Land from the Turks. (2) To protect Constantinople from attack by the Turks. (3) To protect pilgrims and make it safe for them to undertake pilgrimages to the Holy Land.

RESULTS: (1) The Crusades prevented the Mohammedans from gaining control of Europe; they stopped the spread of Mohammedanism in Europe. (2) They failed to free the Holy Land permanently from the Turks. (3) They spread the knowledge of the East to the West, particularly the knowledge of arithmetic, astronomy, and medicine, and the knowledge of the West to the East. (4) They led to an increase of trade between the East and the West. (5) It was the desire of Columbus to find an all-water route to the Indies that brought him to the New World.

PICTURES IN THE CHAPTER

Preaching the Crusade (p. 212). Pope Urban II preaching the First Crusade.

Kings' Crusade (p. 214). In the center is King Richard of England and following him is King Philip Augustus of France.

CHAPTER 16. THE GUARDIAN OF ANCIENT TREASURES

OBJECTIVES

1. To develop a clear concept of the fact that during the Middle Ages the Catholic Church was the most powerful guiding force in the lives of the people.

2. To help children understand that the Church ceaselessly endeavored to abolish warfare and to promote peace between nations and individuals.

3. To give children a clear understanding of the lasting influence of the great men and women of the Middle Ages, such as St. Francis of Assisi, St. Dominic, St. Thomas Aquinas, St. Clare, St. Elizabeth of Hungary, and Blanche of Castile.

4. To arouse a desire to study the character of these great saints, and to see how they can become the models and ideals of everyday life.

5. To develop the children's powers of appreciation and observation, and to help them distinguish the different types of architecture.

Study Tests for Review (pages 230-31)

A. Acceptable answers are:

1. state
2. Elizabeth of Hungary
3-4. Assisi, Italy
5. angry (cross, annoyed)
6. Clare
7. our Lord (Jesus Christ)
8. St. Dominic
9. Blanche of Castile
10. churches
11-12. Gothic, Romanesque
13. Romanesque
14. Gothic

B. The numbers to be inserted in Column B are:

(17) is known as the "Angelic Doctor"
(18) preached in southern France
(16) lived a life of great poverty
(15) forbade fighting during Lent and Advent

Interest may be stimulated if the teacher brings to class pictures of some of the famous cathedrals in Europe, such as Notre Dame, Chartres, and Amiens in France, Cologne in Germany, Prague in Czechoslovakia, Burgos in Spain, and Salisbury and York in England. History may be correlated with geography by locating the place on the map where each cathedral was built and marking it with some symbol, such as a cross. After a certain amount of drill work, the pupils may be asked to located the cathedrals on a wall map or on individual outline maps.

Pictures in the Chapter

Religious Procession (p. 221). In the background is the Church of S. Michele, Pavia, Italy, in the Romanesque style typified by round arches, heavy walls, small window openings.

St. Francis and the Crib of Greccio (p. 223). When St. Francis visited Rome in 1223 he told Pope Honorius II of the plans he had made for making a scenic representation of the place of the Nativity and received the Pope's sanction. He arrived at Greccio on Christmas

Eve and with the aid of a friend constructed a crib and grouped around it figures of the Blessed Virgin, St. Joseph, the shepherds, the ass, the ox. Legend relates that at the midnight Mass, having sung the words of the Gospel "and they laid him in a manger," St. Francis knelt down to meditate briefly on the Incarnation and there appeared in his arms a child surrounded by a brilliant light.

Gothic Cathedral (p. 228). This interior view of a Gothic cathedral shows the pointed arches typical of the architectural style. The large windows were filled with leaded glass in deep, rich colors—largely reds and blues but with some yellows, greens, and "off-whites." The designs of the windows were often patterns of circular, square, or diamond-shaped medallions, in each of which was represented some event in sacred history. The headdress of the woman in the lower right foreground is the type worn by noblewomen in the early fifteenth century, particularly in France. The man in the middle and the woman in the far distance are also in costumes of nobles. The other women wear clothing of the humbler classes.

READING LIST

Chapman, Michael Andrew. *A Garland of Saints for Children.* Frederick Pustet Company, 1929. Contains stories of St. Clare, St. Lawrence, St. Augustine.

Cullen, Margaret R. *Saint Francis of Assisi, the Little Poor Man.* Mission Press, Providence, Rhode Island, 1941. A life of St. Francis written for children.

Ernest, Brother. *The Boy Who Threw Away His Gold.* Dujarie Press, Notre Dame, Indiana, 1943. A life of St. Francis of Assisi.

Lownsbery, Eloise. *The Boy Knight of Reims.* Houghton Mifflin Company, 1927. The story of a boy and his services in the Cathedral of Reims about the time of Charles VII. All of the master workmen of Jean's family had helped in building the cathedral, and his desire to contribute was fulfilled when he was commissioned to make a statue of Joan of Arc for the square.

Maritain, Raissa. *St. Thomas Aquinas, the Angel of the Schools.* Sheed and Ward, 1935. An excellent spiritual book for children.

Melloy, Camille. *Troubadour of God.* P. J. Kenedy and Sons, 1938. A life of St. Francis of Assisi.

Milhous, Katherine. *The First Christmas Crib.* How Francis made the first crib at Greccio to teach the people the meaning of Christ's humble birth.

Windeatt, Mary Fabyan. *Little Sister*. The Grail, St. Meinrad, Indiana, 1944. The story of Blessed Imelda, patroness of first communicants.

Windeatt, Mary Fabyan. *My Name Is Thomas*. The Grail, St. Meinrad, Indiana, 1943. A life of St. Thomas Aquinas.

Windeatt, Mary Fabyan. *Saints in the Sky*. Sheed and Ward, 1941. The story of St. Catherine of Siena.

CHAPTER 17. GREED AND JEALOUSY OVER TREASURES

OBJECTIVES

1. To help children understand that the power of the kings of the European countries increased as a result of the decline of feudalism after the Crusades.

2. To develop an understanding of the growth and development of strong national tendencies which, then as now, resulted in rivalry and war.

3. To emphasize the fact that God does not always choose as His instruments people whom the world would select as strong leaders.

4. To arouse within children's minds a realization that very important events were taking place in Europe at the same time that Columbus discovered America.

STUDY TESTS FOR REVIEW (pages 238-39)[1]

A. Acceptable answers are:

1. Orleans
2-3. Spain, Portugal
4-5. Greenland, Iceland
6. Granada
7-9. Norway, Sweden, Denmark

B. The words to be written in the blank spaces are:

10-11. feudal, kings
12. national
13. Verdun
14. Black Prince
15. Joan of Arc
16. Calais
17. Henry
18. Portuguese
19. Spain
20-21. Germany, Italy

---

[1] It would be a help to a better understanding of history to use a map when preparing this exercise in order to familiarize pupils with the location of the places mentioned. It may be necessary to explain that Spain was made up of several kingdoms until the marriage of Isabella of Castile and Ferdinand of Aragon (1469) united these two kingdoms. Granada was conquered in 1492. See the map on page 236.

C. The words to be underlined are:

22. more
23. cruel
24. more powerful
25. central

PICTURE IN THE CHAPTER

The Departure of Columbus (p. 237). Father Juan Perez, who accompanied Columbus on his second voyage to the New World, blesses Columbus as he departs on the famous voyage that led to the discovery of America.

READING LIST

Boutet de Monvel, Louis Maurice. *Joan of Arc.* Appleton-Century-Crofts, 1907. A beautiful picture-book biography that appeals to readers of any age.

Eaton, Jeanette. *Jeanne d'Arc.* Harper and Brothers, 1931. A small book containing five chapters of swiftly moving narrative that makes the heroine seem like a real person.

Perkins, Lucy Fitch. *The Norwegian Twins.* Houghton Mifflin Company, 1933. The life and experiences of Eric and Elsa on a farm in Norway in the days of long ago.

Snedden, Genevra. *Leif and Thorkel: Two Norse Boys of Long Ago.* World Book Company, 1922. The story of two boys in old Scandinavia. Pictures life of olden days, describes voyages to Greenland and America.

CHAPTER 18. SPREADING TREASURES TO OTHERS

OBJECTIVES

1. To help children realize that each nation or group of peoples has in some way contributed to the development and progress of civilization.

2. To form a clear concept of the effect of the barbarian invasions on this development and progress, and an understanding of the work of the Church in preserving culture and civilization.

3. To help children realize the importance of the Crusades in linking East with West, and to develop an understanding of the renewed interest in the culture of the ancients which was thus aroused.

4. To show why the Renaissance began in Italy.

5. To emphasize the fact that though the Renaissance began in Italy, where many ancient treasures were discovered and where men

had money and leisure to devote to the development of culture, it soon spread to the other countries of Europe.

6. To form a clear concept of the importance of the origin of national languages.

7. To help the child form a true understanding of how the invention of the printing press, the compass, and the astrolabe helped spread knowledge to all places and to all peoples alike.

Study Tests for Review (pages 250-51)

A. Acceptable answers are:

1. Constantinople
2. classics
3. rebirth
4. Italy
5. Leonardo da Vinci
6. Michelangelo
7. Raphael
8. Michelangelo
9. Dante
10. the printing press
11. John Gutenberg
12. the compass

B. The correct answers are:

13. True   14. True   15. False   16. False

Who's Who in the Later Middle Ages

Person	Nation	Important Fact
Black Prince	England	A famous leader of the English during the Hundred Years' War
Blanche of Castile	France	A very holy woman, the mother of King Louis IX (St. Louis) of France
St. Clare	Italy	A noble Italian lady who became the first Franciscan sister
Dante	Italy	The great Italian poet who wrote the *Divine Comedy*
St. Dominic	Spain	A Spaniard who founded the Dominicans, known as the Order of Preachers
St. Elizabeth	Hungary	The daughter of King Andrew of Hungary, who loved the poor and worked hard to help them
St. Francis of Assisi	Italy	A very lovable saint of the Middle Ages who established the Franciscan order

Person	Nation	Important Fact
Frederick Barbarossa	Germany	A king of Germany who went on the Third Crusade
John Gutenberg	Germany	Invented the printing press
Prince Henry	Portugal	Gave all his time and money to the study of navigation
St. Joan of Arc	France	The Maid of Orleans, who led the French armies to victory in the Hundred Years' War
Kublai Khan	China	The ruler of Cathay (China) in the days of Marco Polo
King Louis IX	France	The saintly king who went on two crusades to the Holy Land
Michelangelo	Italy	The great Renaissance artist who designed the dome of St. Peter's in Rome and carved famous statues
Peter the Hermit	France	Led an unorganized expedition to the Holy Land, but it was a complete failure
Marco Polo	Italy	A famous Venetian who lived for a long time in China and wrote about all the wealth and treasures of the Orient
Raphael	Italy	A Renaissance artist who is famous for his Madonnas
Saladin	Turks	The leader of the Turks during the Crusades
Pope Urban II	France	Urged the people of western Europe to organize the Crusades
Leonardo da Vinci	Italy	A Renaissance artist who painted the well-known picture of the Last Supper

Pictures in the Chapter

Life in the Renaissance Period (p. 241). Note the magnificent buildings and clothing worn by the nobility of this period. An artist is here presenting a painting to his patron for the latter's approval.

St. Peter's Basilica (p. 242). To realize the great size of this building note the size of the people in the piazza and on the steps.

Early Printing Shop (p. 247). The man at right is setting type, the master of the shop examines the proof, and the man at the left operates the press. Wet impressions hang on strings to dry.

READING LIST

De la Ramée, Louise. *A Dog of Flanders*. The Macmillan Company, 1925. The story of the little Flemish boy Nello and his faithful dog Patrasche. The boy's love for Ruben's paintings is shown in the story.

Deucher, Sybil and Wheeler, Opal. *Giotto Tended the Sheep*. E. P. Dutton and Company, 1938. Beautiful format with many illustrations and reproductions of three of Giotto's masterpieces, including "St. Francis of Assisi."

Gilchrist, Marie Emilie and Ogle, Lucille. *Rolling Along through the Centuries*. Longmans, Green and Company, 1937. The evolution of land travel, from the making of wheels in primitive times to modern streamline trains and automobiles. Profusely illustrated.

McMurtrie, Douglas Crawford and Farran, Don. *Wings for Words*. Rand McNally and Company, 1940. An interesting, moving, and graphic account of Johann Gutenberg and the invention of printing.

SEMESTER TEST

[Based on material covered in Chapters 8-18]

A. Before each item in Column B write the number of the item in Column A which is most closely connected with it.

Column A	Column B
1. Alaric	( ) defeated the Mohammedans in 732 A.D.
2. St. Augustine of Hippo	( ) designed the dome of St. Peter's
3. Rollo	( ) brave leader of the English in the Hundred Years' War
4. Charles Martel	( ) leader of the Visigoths who sacked Rome
5. John Gutenberg	( ) famous leader of the Northmen
6. Michelangelo	( ) French king who went on two crusades
7. Mohammed	( ) invented the printing press
8. William the Conqueror	( ) once a sinner, he became a great saint
9. St. Louis	( ) founder of a new religion
10. Black Prince	( ) made a successful invasion of England

B. Underline the words in parentheses which complete correctly the following sentences.

11. Attila was the leader of the (Normans, Huns, Franks).
12. The greatest of the Carolingian kings was (Clovis, Charles Martel, Charlemagne).
13. The "Apostle of the Germans" was (St. Boniface, St. Cyril, St. Augustine).
14. The Mohammedan religion was founded in (India, China, Arabia).
15. St. Clare was the first (Dominican, Franciscan, Benedictine) sister.
16. St. Cyril and St. Methodius preached to the (Irish, French, Slavs).
17. In feudal times the members of the ruling class were called (vassals, fiefs, lords).
18. Feudal castles were surrounded by (an iron fence, a moat, a stone wall).
19. The first stage in the training of a boy in feudal days was that of a (knight, page, squire).
20. Cathay is another name for (India, China, Japan).
21. Flanders is that part of Europe which we call (Denmark, Switzerland, Belgium).
22. We speak of (St. Francis, St. Dominic, St. Thomas Aquinas) as the "Angelic Doctor."
23. The Hundred Years' War was fought between England and (Spain, Germany, France).
24. Ferdinand and Isabella were king and queen of (England, France, Spain).
25. The "Mona Lisa" was painted by (Raphael, da Vinci, Michelangelo).

C. Complete the following sentences by writing the correct word in each of the blank spaces.

26. The sacred book of the Mohammedans is the ....
27. St. Benedict called the Divine Office the ....
28. The famous monastery of Monte Cassino in Italy was built by ....
29. The large empire of Charlemagne was divided among his three grandsons by the Treaty of ....

30. In feudal times a battle fought between pairs of knights was called a ....

31. The only English king who has had the title of "Great" is ....

32. The most important trading center of the Middle Ages was the Italian city of ....

33. The Second Crusade was preached by ....

34. The great leader of the Saracens during the Crusades was ....

35. The Order of Preachers was founded by ....

36. Cathedrals with large stained glass windows and tall graceful spires are called .... cathedrals.

37. The "Maid of Orleans" is another name for ....

38. The frescoes on the ceiling of the Sistine Chapel in the Vatican were painted by ....

39. The *Divine Comedy* was written by ....

40. The first printing press set up outside of Germany was that of the .... monks near Rome.

D. Write on the dotted line to the right of each item the date, chosen from the list, in which the event took place.

597	732	843	1095	1453
622	800	1066	1400	1492

41. Charles Martel defeated the Moors in the Battle of Tours. ....

42. William, duke of Normandy, invaded England. ....

43. The first year in the Mohammedan calendar. ....

44. The Mohammedans were driven from Granada in Spain. ....

45. Pope Urban II urged the Christians of western Europe to free the Holy Land from the Turks. ....

46. The Hundred Years' War came to an end. ....

47. The year in which John Gutenberg was born. ....

48. St. Augustine began his missionary labors in England. ....

49. Charlemagne was proclaimed emperor of the Romans. ....

50. Charlemagne's empire was divided into three separate kingdoms. ....

E. Complete the following sentences by filling in the blank spaces with words taken from this list. A word may be used more than once if necessary; some may not be used at all.

Mediterranean Sea	Germany	English Channel
Adriatic Sea	Italy	Rhine River
Black Sea	France	Indus River
North Sea	Spain	Loire River

51. Venice, a city of northern Italy, is on the ....
52. Marseilles, a seaport of France, is on the ....
53. Barcelona is a Mediterranean port in ....
54. Cologne is an important city in ....
55. The .... separates England from France.
56. Normandy is in the northern part of ....
57. The Papal States were in central ....
58. The Danes crossed the .... to invade England.
59. Mohammedan armies made conquests as far east as the .... in India.
60. The Franks lived on the borders of the .... in what is today part of Germany.

F. Before each item in Column B write the number of the item in Column A which is most closely connected with it.

Column A	Column B
61. Danelaw	( ) a period of renewed interest in the works of the ancient Greeks and Romans
62. Salisbury Oath	( ) the name given to a young boy who was learning a trade
63. Domesday Book	( ) a form of government during the Middle Ages
64. Truce of God	( ) greatly strengthened the power of William the Conqueror after he became king of England
65. Black Death	( ) the blow on the back of the neck given during ceremony of knighthood
66. Renaissance	( ) forbade fighting during Advent and Lent
67. feudalism	( ) a horrible disease that spread far and wide during the Hundred Years' War
68. chivalry	( ) a part of Britain settled by the Danes
69. accolade	( ) the first census taken in England
70. apprentice	( ) the name given to the rules which formed a knightly code of manners

G. Important peoples of the Middle Ages are listed in Column A. Before each item in Column B write the number of the peoples with which the event is most closely connected.

Column A	Column B
71. Portuguese	( ) were converted to Christianity under leadership of Clovis
72. Northmen	( ) were led to victory in the Hundred Years' War by Joan of Arc
73. Saracens	( ) drove the Danes into the northern part of Britain
74. Danes	( ) were the first to make a successful voyage around the southern tip of Africa
75. Anglo-Saxons	( ) were Turks who held possession of the Holy Land
76. Italians	( ) were the strong, adventurous people who settled on the coasts of France, England, and Italy
77. Spaniards	( ) sacked Rome during the time of Pope Leo I
78. Franks	( ) conquered England during the reign of "Ethelred the Unready"
79. Vandals	( ) helped Columbus in his search for a new trade route to the East
80. French	( ) were the first great artists of the Renaissance

H. On the line after each name write the name of the country, or countries, chosen from the list, with which each is most closely connected. The name of any country may be used more than once if necessary.

| Italy | Portugal | England | China | Spain |
| France | Arabia | Germany | Hungary | Denmark |

81. St. Augustine of Canterbury ....
82. King Canute ....
83. St. Benedict ....
84. St. Louis ....
85. Prince Henry the Navigator ....
86. St. Elizabeth ....
87. Marco Polo ....
88. Kublai Khan ....

89. St. Dominic ....
90. Black Prince ....

I. Write the answers to the following questions in the blank spaces at the right.

91. What is sometimes called man's greatest invention? ....

92. What is the name given to that period of history between the fall of the Roman Empire in the West and the discovery of America? ....

93. Who was the prince against whom William the Conqueror fought in the Battle of Hastings? ....

94. Who is called the "Father of Western Monasticism"? ....

95. Which city in Arabia was the birthplace of Mohammed? ....

96. Who was the ancient monk who lived as a hermit? ....

97. Where was the original home of the Huns? ....

98. What was the name given to groups of merchants who worked together to make arrangements for journeys? ....

99. What was the one English possession in France after the Hundred Years' War? ....

100. What European country other than Italy was not a leading nation at the end of the Middle Ages? ....

Answers to Semester Test

A. The numbers to be inserted in Column B are:

(4) defeated the Mohammedans in 732 A.D.
(6) designed the dome of St. Peter's
(10) brave leader of the English in the Hundred Years' War
(1) leader of the Visigoths who sacked Rome
(3) famous leader of the Northmen
(9) French king who went on two crusades
(5) invented the printing press
(2) once a sinner, he became a great saint
(7) founder of a new religion
(8) made a successful invasion of England

B. The words to be underlined are:

11. Huns	14. Arabia	17. lords
12. Charlemagne	15. Franciscan	18. a moat
13. St. Boniface	16. Slavs	19. page

20. China   22. St. Thomas Aquinas   24. Spain
21. Belgium   23. France   25. da Vinci

C. The words to be written in the blank spaces are:

26. Koran   31. Alfred the Great   36. Gothic
27. "work of God"   32. Venice   37. Joan of Arc
28. St. Benedict   33. St. Bernard   38. Michelangelo
    (the Benedictines)   34. Saladin   39. Dante
29. Verdun   35. St. Dominic   40. Benedictine
30. joust

D. The correct dates are:

41. 732   43. 622   45. 1095   47. 1400   49. 800
42. 1066   44. 1492   46. 1453   48. 597   50. 843

E. The words to be written in the blank spaces are:

51. Adriatic Sea   54. Germany   58. North Sea
52. Mediterranean   55. English Channel   59. Indus River
    Sea   56. France   60. Rhine River
53. Spain   57. Italy

F. The numbers to be inserted in Column B are:

(66) a period of renewed interest in the works of the ancient Greeks and Romans
(70) the name given to a young boy who was learning a trade
(67) a form of government during the Middle Ages
(62) greatly strengthened the power of William the Conqueror after he became king of England
(69) the blow on the back of the neck given during the ceremony of knighthood
(64) forbade fighting during Advent and Lent
(65) a horrible disease that spread far and wide during the Hundred Years' War
(61) a part of Britain settled by the Danes
(63) the first census taken in England
(68) the name given to the rules which formed a knightly code of manners

G. The numbers to be inserted in Column B are:

(78) were converted to Christianity under the leadership of Clovis
(80) were led to victory in the Hundred Years' War by Joan of Arc
(75) drove the Danes into the northern part of Britain

(71) were the first to make a successful voyage around the southern tip of Africa
(73) were Turks who held possession of the Holy Land
(72) were the strong, adventurous people who settled on the coasts of France, England, and Italy
(79) sacked Rome during the time of Pope Leo I
(74) conquered England during the reign of "Ethelred the Unready"
(77) helped Columbus in his search for a new trade route to the East
(76) were the first great artists of the Renaissance

H. The countries to be named are:

81. England
82. England, Denmark
83. Italy
84. France
85. Portugal
86. Hungary
87. China, Italy (Venice)
88. China
89. France, Spain
90. England, France

I. The words to be written in the blank spaces are:

91. printing press
92. Middle Ages
93. Harold
94. St. Benedict
95. Mecca
96. St. Anthony
97. central Asia
98. guilds, merchant guilds
99. Calais
100. Germany

WORKBOOK ANSWER KEY

Let's Get Acquainted – Page 1

1. in the front of our book
2. Our Greatest Treasure
3. 18
4. 149
5. in the back of our book
6. Doom z'da
7. boo
8. after
9. in the back of our book
10. p. 57
11. p. 173, 174, 237
12. p. 184

Learning About the Past – Page 3

1. yes
2. no
3. no
4. yes
5. yes
6. no
7. yes
8. no
9. yes
10. yes

Ancient Egypt – Page 4

1. black land
2. flood
3. fertile
4. linen
5. sowing of the seed
6. calendar
7. flood time
8. red land

9. harvest
10. papyrus
11. Mediterranean
12. Arabian
13. Red
14. Rosetta
15. Euphrates
16. mêd-î-te-ra-ne-ân;
17. sa-här-á
18. ro-zêt-á
19. ti-grîs
20. u-fra-tez

The Egyptians – Page 6

1. 4
2. 6
3. 9
4. 3
5. 8
6. 2
7. 10
8. 1
9. 7
10. 5
11. mason
12. architect
13. goldsmith, jeweler
14. Scribes
15. waterman
16. E
17. U
18. E-U
19. E
20. E-U
21. E
22. There are no slaves. U
23. Pillows are made of wood or stone. E
24. Mirrors are made of glass. U
25. E-U

The Babylonians – Page 8

1. B
2. A
3. B
4. Y
5. L
6. O
7. N
8. W
9. A
10. S
11. T
12. H
13. E
14. C
15. A
16. P
17. I
18. T
19. A
20. L

Sentence at bottom: "Babylon was the capital."

Other Peoples of the Ancient East – Page 9

1. 6
2. C
3. 1
4. A
5-6. 5, 4
7. 3
8-9. D, E
10. B
11. north
12. twenty-two
13. Saul
14. Nineveh
15. Carthage
16. Hebrews
17. their king had all the power
18. cedar
19. warlike

20. knowledge of the one true God
21. keep a strong army and navy
22. Jerusalem
23. Nineveh
24. Psalms
25. Tigris

Greece and Sparta – Page 11

1. soldiers
2. rivers
3. helots
4-5. Athens, Sparta
6. Europe
7. peninsula
8. southern
9. seven
10. mountains
11. severe or harsh
12. Mediterranean Sea
13-14. Spartans, Athenians
15. two

Athens – Page 12

1. true
2. true
3. true
4. false
5. false
6. true
7. false
8. true
9. true
10. false
11. G
12. A
13. G
14. S
15. A
16. G

17. A
18. S
19. S
20. A

The Treasures of the Greeks – Page 14

1. Alexander the Great
2. Pericles
3. Acropolis
4. Demosthenes
5. Socrates
6. Parthenon
7. Herodotus
8. Phidias
9. Homer
10. Leonidas
11. Olympic Games
12. Marathon
13. King Philip of Macedon
14. Apollo
15. Democracy
16. Mt. Olympus
17-18. Crete, Cyprus
19. South
20. Aegean
21. Thermoplyae
22. Macedonia
23. Troy
24. Egypt
25. Asia Minor

Rome and the Romans – Page 16

1. yes
2. yes
3. yes
4. no
5. no
6. yes
7. yes
8. no

9. yes
10. no
11. 13
12. 18
13. 15
14. 11
15. 20
16. 12
17. 19
18. 14
19. 16
20. 17

Roman Wars and Roman Rulers – Page 18

1. France
2. Pompey
3. Augustus
4. Cassius and Brutus
5. Punic Wars
6. Vergil and Horace
7. birth of Christ
8. emperor
9. Phoenicians
10. England
11. The Tarquins ruled Rome
12. Carthage was destroyed
13. Julius Caesar
14. Julius Caesar was born
15. Hannibal invaded Italy
16. Alps (Mountain)
17. Tiber (River)
18. Carthage (City)
19. Apernine Pyranees (Mountain)
20. Mediterranean (Sea)
21. Adriatic (Sea)
22. Syracuse (City)
23. Pyranees (Mountain)
24. Naples (City)
25. Po (River)

Review – Page 20

1. 5
2. 9
3. 4
4. 1
5. 8
6. 2
7. 6
8. 10
9. 3
10. 7
11. Hellenistic
12. hieroglyphics
13. papyrus
14. Augustus
15-16. Parthenon, Acropolis
17-18. Romulus, Remus
19-20. Tiberius and Gaius Gracchus
 (**2** brothers, any order, p. 71)
21. Rome
22-23. Italy, Greece
24-25. Cassius, Brutus
26. Euphrates
27. an island
28. sculptor
29. flax
30. cuneiform writing
31. Greeks
32. Colosseum
33. Zeus
34. Pyramids
35. held their thumbs down
36. Moses
37. Herodotus
38. black
39. ships
40. Solomon
41. King Philip of Macedon
42. Emperor Vespasian
43. obelisk
44. Macedonia
45. Carthage

46. Homer
47. Patricians
48. Sparta
49. Nile
50. Sphinx
51. Hebrews
52. Assyrians
53. Babylonians
54. Romans
55. Phoenicians
56. Hebrews
57. Assyrians
58. Persians
59. Egyptians
60. Greeks
61. Phoenicians
62. Greeks
63. Persians
64. Romans
65. Babylonians
66. 68
67. 69
68. 66
69. 74
70. 75
71. 70
72. 67
73. 71
74. 72
75. 73
76. true
77. false
78. true
79. true
80. false
81. true
82. false
83. true
84. true
85. false
86. true
87. true
88. false

89. true
90. false
91. Mesopotamia
92. Tiber
93. Italy
94. Alps
95. Tigris
96. Africa
97. Mediterranean
98. Adriatic
99. Africa
100. Po

Our Greatest Treasure – Page 25

1. St. John
2. Bethlehem
3. Jesus Christ
4. Rome
5. Jerusalem
6. Nazareth
7. Garden of Olives
8. 3 hours

9-10. obedience and love

11. 14
12. 13
13. 15
14. 11
15. 12
16. angels
17. Jesus
18. Angel Gabriel
19. Blessed Virgin Mary
20. Jesus

The Founding of the Church – Page 27

1. false
2. true
3. true
4. false
5. true
6. true

7. false
8. true
9. true
10. false
11. 13
12. 15
13. 18
14. 11
15. 16
16. 19
17. 12
18. 20
19. 17
20. 14

The Early Church – Page 29

1. St. Agnes
2. St. Lawrence
3. St. Peter
4. St. Tarcisius
5. St. Felicitas
6. Christians were buried in the catacombs
7. The first Mass was offered
8. St. Peter began to preach in public
9. Emperor Nero persecuted the Christians
10. Emperor Constantine defeated Maxentius in battle
11. ended the persecution of the Christians
12. Theodosius
13. martyr
14. all nations
15. St. Sebastian
16. persecutions
17. A.D. 313
18. beheaded
19. Theodosius
20. at peace
21. Jews
22. the burning of Rome
23. Scriptures to be burned
24. catacombs
25. Christians

Treasures from the Romans – Page 31

1. 4
2. 8
3. 6
4. 2
5. 7
6. 3
7. 1
8. 5
9. the Romans built fine roads
10. all the lands along the shores of the Mediterranean Sea
11. was a great lawgiver
12. Augustus
13. their soldiers
14. blood of martyrs
15. the people
16. are still in use today
17. people of many different races
18. throughout the Roman Empire
19. his letters
20. preserved Greek civilization and learning

The End of the Roman Empire – Page 34

1. true
2. true
3. true
4. true
5. false
6. true
7. false
8. false
9. true
10. false
11. false
12. true
13. true
14. false
15. true
16. eight
17. Carthage
18. Adriatic Sea

19. Atlantic Sea
20. Milan
21. Alexandria
22. London
23. Danube River
24. Black Sea
25. Damascus

Review – Page 36

1. 6
2. 3
3. 4
4. 7
5. 9
6. 2
7. 10
8. 5
9. 8
10. 1
11. Incarnation
12. Asia
13. Catacombs
14. Canon
15. Constantinople
16-17. Jerusalem, Pasch
18. Pentecost/Whitsunday
19. Bethlehem
20. the Pope
21. Damascus
22. Justinian
23. Martyr
24. Nazareth
25. Mediterranean
26. Christ
27. Messias
28. A.D. 313
29. Lazarus
30. western
31. gentiles
32. fine roads
33. He would rise from the dead
34. Provinces

35. 476
36. Judas
37. St. Peter
38. Augustus
39. St. Paul
40. St. John
41. Cicero
42. Mary Magdalene
43. St. Lawrence
44. St. Peter
45. Longinus
46. false
47. true
48. false
49. false
50. false
51. true
52. false
53. true
54. true
55. true
56. false
57. true
58. false
59. true
60. true

The Huns and the Barbarians – Page 39

1. Huns
2. Germans
3. Romans
4. Germans
5. Romans
6. Germans
7. Huns
8. Romans
9. Huns
10. Germans
11. yes
12. no
13. yes
14. yes

15. yes
16. no
17. yes
18. yes
19. no
20. yes
21. no
22. no
23. no
24. no
25. no

The Franks – Page 41

1. Pepin
2. St. Remi
3. Clotilde
4. Clovis
5. St. Boniface
6. Rhine
7. St. Remi
8. Charlemagne
9-10. Arabs, Tours
11. Ministers of the Frankish kings
12. "do nothing kings"
13. Pepin
14. Clovis
15. Catholic
16. Continent
17. River
18. City
19. River
20. Continent
21. River
22. Island
23. Continent
24. City
25. Island

Mohammed and His Teachings – Page 43

1. 4
2. 5
3. 8
4. 10
5. 7
6. 9
7. 2
8. 6
9. 3
10. 1
11. north
12. five times
13. by marriage
14. one god
15. Mecca
16. Arabia
17. won many battles
18. Mecca
19. sometimes fainthearted
20. 570

Mohammedan Conquests – Page 44

1. Tours, 5
2. Medina, 2
3. Spain, 4
4. Mecca, 1
5. Red Sea, 3
6. true
7. true
8. false
9. true
10. false
11. false
12. true
13. false
14. false
15. true

The First Monks – Page 46

1. 4
2. 5
3. 2
4. 1
5. 3
6. they wanted to give themselves entirely to God
7. poverty, chastity, and obedience
8. St. Anthony
9. Egypt
10. nine monasteries for men and two for women
11. were permitted to plan their day as they chose
12. had to do some kind of work
13. they do not all live in a monastery as a family
14. they have not all received the sacrament of Holy Orders

Two Great Saints – Page 48

1. A
2. P
3. P
4. A
5. P
6. A
7. A
8. P
9. A
10. P
11. false
12. false
13. true
14. false, true, either answer, the book does not say
15. true
16. true
17. false
18. false
19. true
20. True

St. Benedict – Page 50

1-2. hermit, Rome
3. climate
4. pray
5. a rule
6. monks
7. preserved
8. together
9. the father or head of a religious family
10. Divine office
11. Italy
12. gaining
13. copying
14. civilization
15. offering our work to God

Famous Missionaries – Page 51

1. St. Boniface
2-3. St. Methodius, St. Cyril
4. St. Patrick
5. Bertha
6. St. Augustine of Canterbury
7. St. Augustine of Hippo
8. Julius Caesar
9. St. Methodius
10. St. Gregory the Great
11. yes
12. no
13. no
14. yes
15. no
16. yes
17. yes
18. no
19. yes
20. no
21. yes
22. yes
23. no
24. no
25. no

Review – Page 53

1. 5
2. 8
3. 10
4. 62
5. 1
6. 9
7. 3
8. 4
9. 7
10. St. Benedict
11. Seminary
12. St. Boniface
13. St. Patrick
14. Mosque
15. monastery
17-18. Mohammed, Medina
19. Leo 1
20. Koran
21. Charles Martel
22. St. Benedict
23. Moors
24-25. St. Cyril, St. Methodius
26. false
27. true
28. true
29. true
30. false
31. false
32. true
33. false
34. true
35. false
36. true
37. true
38. false
39. true
40. false
41. Franks
42. North
43. St. Pachomius
44. Charles Martel

45. St. Boniface
46. Gregory the Great
47. Pepin
48. hermit
49. Mohammedans
50. an abbot
51. Visigoths
52. civilized
53. St. Augustine of Canterbury
54. Alaric
55. Rome
56. Italy
57. Africa
58. England
59. Italy
60. France
61. England
62. Italy
63. France
64. Arabia
65. France

Charlemagne – Page 56

1. false
2. true
3. false
4. false
5. true
6. true
7. true
8. false
9. true
10. true
11. false
12. false
13. false
14. true
15. true
16. true
17. false
18. true
19. true

20. true
21. false
22. true
23. false
24. false
25. true

After the Death of Charlemagne – Page 58

1. 2
2. 4
3. 1
4. 5
5. 3
6. east
7. Vikings
8. Normans
9. south
10. Lombards
11. Lotharingia
12. Rome
13. East Frankland
14. English Channel
15. West Frankland
16-17. Cross out Pepin; Pepin was not one of the sons of Charlemagne. Pepin was the Father of Charlemagne.
18-19. Cross out Hungarians; The Hungarians were a group that came from the East. The other three all came from the North.
20-21. Cross out England; England is not one of the kingdoms into which Charlemagne's territory was divided.
22-23. Cross out France; France was not a country from which the barbaric tribes tried to conquer the territory that Charlemagne's land was divided into.
24-25. Cross out Irish; The Irish did not have a group of barbaric people that tried to conquer or hurt others.

King Alfred the Great – Page 61

1. separate kingdoms
2. Danelaw
3. Wessex
4. live in peace with the other people in Britain
5. only
6. record of events
7. same language
8. Danes
9. Britain
10. King Alfred
11. Anglo-Saxon
12. an island
13. North
14. almost destroyed
15-16. Saxons, twenty-three
17. Alfred
18. Wessex
19. Anglo-Saxon
20. protect his own kingdom from the Danes

The Norman Conquest – Page 62

1. William the Conqueror
2. Harold
3. William the Conqueror
4. Alfred
5. Canute
6. Alfred
7. William the Conqueror
8. William the Conqueror
9. Alfred
10. Ethelred
11. Harold
12. Edward
13. Harold
14. William the Conqueror
15. Ethelred
16. Wessex-6
17. English Channel-10
18. Normandy-4
19. Denmark-8

20. Canterbury-7
21. North Sea-9
22. Hastings-1
23. Danelaw-5
24. London-3
25. Paris-2

Feudalism – Page 64

1. vassal
2. vassal
3. vassal
4. serfs
5. lord
6. vassal
7. serf
8. vassal
9. lord
10. vassal
11. no
12. yes
13. no
14. no
15. no
16. yes
17. no
18. yes
19. yes
20. no
21. no
22. no
23. no
24. yes
25. yes

Knights and Chivalry – Page 66

1. accolade
2. page
3. squire
4. run errands for the ladies
5. loyal
6. horse

7. unarmed
8. knight
9. simple
10. at the court of some nobleman
11. armor
12. lance
13. shield
14. mail
15. weapons
16. sword
17-18. steel, cone
19. chivalry
20. soldier

Life in the Castles – Page 68

1. true
2. false
3. false
4. true
5. true
6. feudalism
7. entertainment
8. use of weapons
9. dangerous
10. accolade
11. lords
12. landholder
13. oath of fealty
14. ransom
15. ditch
16. squire
17. linen
18. invention of gunpowder
19. vassals
20. eldest son
21. drawbridge
22. inherited
23. nobles
24. chivalry
25. arms
26. serfs
27. tower

28. lance
29. earth
30. Sword
Answer to puzzle: *Feudal lords lived in castles*

Merchant of the Middles Ages – Page 70

1-3. apprentice, journeyman, master
4. Medieval fairs
5. Spain
6-8. Genoa, Pisa, Venice
9. day
10. merchant
11. journeymen
12. Marseilles
13. Adriatic
14. Mohammedans
15. woolen
16. masterpiece
17. profitable
18. craft
19-20. wages, guild
21. Mcditcrranean
22. England
23-24. Constantinople, Marseilles
25. Apprentice

The Travels of Marco Polo – Page 71

1. Marco Polo visited Cipango
2. Kublai Khan asked the Pope to send missionaries to his country
3. The Polos returned to Venice
4. The family and friends of the Polos did not recognize them
5. Marco Polo's mother died
6. 8
7. 14
8. 9
9. 11
10. 15
11. 13
12. 6
13. 10
14. 7

15. 12

Review – Page 73

1. 5
2. 1
3. 7
4. 8
5. 9
6. 4
7. 10
8. 3
9. 2
10. 6
11. Charlemagne
12-13. William I, Harold
14. Kublai Khan
15. Verdun
16. Middle Ages
17-19. Sweden, Norway, Denmark
20. Charles
21. Wessex
22. 1066
23-24. page, squire
25. homage
26. merchant
27. an apprentice
28. Doomsday book
29. Adriatic
30. east
31. Salisbury
32. Spain
33. tournament
34. fief
35. Danelaw
36. knight
37. France
38. Edward
39. Genoa
40. Alfred the Great
41. true
42. false
43. false

44. true
45. true
46. false
47. true
48. true
49. true
50. true
51. false
52. false
53. false
54. true
55. false
56. China
57. England or Angleland would be correct
58. Japan
59. France
60. Germany
61. Belgium
62. Charlemagne
63. Norseman/Northmen
64. Saxons
65. Franks
66. Joust or Tournaments (either would be correct)
67. moat
68. Ethelred
69. Papal States
70. tower

The Crusades – Page 77

1. Pope Urban II
2. knights
3. crusaders
4. Godfrey of Bouillon
5. a cross of cloth
6. 1096-1270
7. a group of pilgrims
8. a complete failure
9. infidels
10. Christianity
11. First crusade
12. pilgrims
13. they planned to attack Constantinople

14. never reached Jerusalem
15. drive the Turks out of the Holy Land.

The End of the Crusades – Page 80

1. Third
2. Kings'
3. Saracens
4. two
5. France
6. Germany
7. the Orient
8. Mohammedans
9. Frederick Barbarossa
10. trade between East and West increased
11. recaptured Jerusalem in 1187
12. France
13. Richard the Lionhearted
14. never reached the Holy Land
15. First
16. Constantinople
17. Mediterranean
18. Jerusalem
19. Barcelona
20. Cologne
21. Venice
22. Austria
23. Alexandria
24. Constantinople
25. Mediterranean

The Church in the Middle Ages – Page 82

1. true
2. true
3. false
4. false
5. true
6. 15
7. 9
8. 13
9. 6
10. 14

11. 12
12. 7
13. 8
14. 11
15. 10
16. 17
17. 19
18. 20
19. 16
20. 18
21. The Church
22. Blanch of Castile
23. Catholic
24. Italy
25. poverty
26. Dominican
27. St. Clare
28. St. Thomas Aquinas
29. Churches/Cathedrals
30. King Louis IX

The Hundred Years' War – Page 84

1. 4
2. 1
3. 5
4. 3
5. 2
6. The Crusades started
7. The Hundred Years' War began
8. Joan of Arc was burned at the stake
9. A French lord became king of England
10. St. Michael appeared in a vision to Joan of Arc
11. The French kings ruled a little land around Paris
12. The Black Prince defeated the French in a very famous battle
13. Feudal lords governed most of France
14. Harold was defeated at the Battle of Hastings
15. The Treaty of Verdun was signed

New Leaders in the Family of Nations – Page 86

1. false
2. true
3. false
4. false
5. true
6. true
7. true
8. false
9. true
10. false
11. true
12. true
13. true
14. false
15. true
16. false
17. true
18. true
19. false
20. false
21. Calais
22. Ireland
23. Germany
24. France
25. Denmark
26. Baltic Sea
27. York
28. Turkish Empire
29. Norway
30. Italy

The Renaissance – Page 88

1. Michelangelo
2. Dante
3. Raphael
4. Michelangelo
5. Church
6. Italy
7. rebirth
8. crusades
9-10. Greeks, Romans

11. Renaissance
12-14. Homer, Cicero, Vergil
15. Shepherds
16. Divine Comedy
17. Latin
18. Leonardo da Vinci
19. painters
20. Vatican
21. Turks
22-23. Towns, trade
24. Italy
25. Italy

Inventions of the Middle Ages – Page 90

1. Benedictine
2. astrolabe
3. printing press
4. Bible
5. lapidary
6. they were made from type
7. parchment
8. equator
9. rags
10-12. 1400, Rhine, Germany
13. lead
14. compass
15. paper
16. sailors
17. expensive
18. were encouraged to continue writing
19. carried the secret of the printing press to other cities
20. land and money

Review – Page 91

1. 6
2. 8
3. 9
4. 7
5. 10
6. 1
7. 5

8. 3
9. 2
10. 4
11. Crusades
12. Portugal
13-14. French, English
15. Pilgrimages
16. rebirth
17. Granada
18. printing press
19. Spain
20. Leonardo da Vinci
21. Third
22. Parchment
23. compass
24. lapidary
25. Portuguese
26. false
27. true
28. false
29. false
30. false
31. true
32. false
33. true
34. true
35. true
36. false
37. true
38. false
39. true
40. true
41. Joan of Arc
42. St. Elizabeth of Hungary
43. Giorgione
44. St. Francis of Assisi
45. St. Thomas Aquinas
46. Godfrey of Bouillon
47. Michelangelo
48. Joan of Arc
49. Saladin
50. Calais
51. St. Elizabeth

52. Jerusalem
53. Joan of Arc
54. St. Bernard
55. Pope Urban II
56. St. Joan of Arc
57. Third
58. England
59. Dominicans
60. central
61. Bible
62. Christ
63. Pyrenees
64. Italian
65. Gothic
66. Mohammedans
67. Germany
68. Ferdinand
69. Dominican
70. Crusaders
71. Christopher Columbus
72. the compass
73. Calais
74. Constantinople
75. Cicero
76. Classics
77. Crusaders or Crusades
78. Catholic
79. Cathedral
80. Cathay (China)

Quarter Exam Answer Keys
(Exams are located in the St. Jerome School Lesson Plan books)

First Quarter Exam Answer Key
(30 points)

Fill in the blanks
1. History
2. fire
3. government
4. Nile
5. 365
6. Rosetta
7. "Black Land"
8. astronomers
9. Babylonians
10. David

Matching Column A/Column B:
(3) stylus
(4) Alexander the Great
(6) Hellenistic
(8) simple
(9) Demosthenes
(2) cedar
(10) Europe
(7) Peninsula
(5) Herodotus
(1) cuneiform writing

Yes or no
1. yes
2. no
3. yes
4. yes
5. yes
6. yes

7. no
8. no
9. yes
10. yes

Second Quarter Exam Answer Key
(30 points)

Fill in the blanks
1. Christ
2. St. Joseph
3. 3
4. Lazarus
5. Olives
6. Commandments
7. Mary Magdalen
8. St. Peter
9. Pentecost
10. Paul

Matching Column A/Column B
(2) Diocletian
(10) Constantine
(7) Cicero
(8) Justinian
(9) Huns
(3) catacombs
(6) Latin
(4) St. Paul
(5) Nero
(1) St. Ambrose

Yes or no
1. no
2. yes
3. no
4. yes
5. no
6. yes
7. yes
8. no
9. yes
10. yes

Third Quarter Exam Answer Key
(35 points)

Fill in the blanks
1. Red Sea
2. Arabs
3. America
4. monks, nuns
5. abbot
6. St. Anthony
7. St. Augustine
8. St. Monica
9. St. Ambrose
10. St. Patrick

Matching Column A/Column B
(3) St. Benedict
(8) Moravian Empire
(6) St. Boniface
(7) St. Cyril & St. Methodius
(9) Charlemagne
(10) Papal States
(1) Ireland
(4) Bertha, a Frankish princess
(5) Canterbury
(2) seminary

Yes or no
1. yes
2. yes
3. yes
4. no
5. yes
6. no
7. no
8. no
9. no
10. yes
11. yes
12. no

13. yes
14. no
15. yes

Fourth Quarter Exam Answer Key
(35 points)

Fill in the blanks
1. merchants
2. guilds
3. Italy
4. Marco Polo
5. Venice
6. Crusades
7. Turks
8. knights
9. children
10. Turks

Matching Column A/Column B
(12) John Gutenberg
(11) Michelangelo
(3) Richard the Lion-hearted
(5) Frederick Barbarossa
(6) Godfrey of Bouillon
(2) Saladin
(10) St. Dominic
(9) St. Thomas Aquinas
(8) The Truce of God
(1) "God wills it"
(7) St. Bernard
(4) Philip Augustus

Yes or no
1. no
2. yes
3. no
4. no
5. yes
6. yes
7. yes
8. no
9. yes
10. no

11. yes
12. yes
13. no
14. yes
15. yes

Printed in Great Britain
by Amazon